Wait and See

by
Scott Kriner

INFINITY
PUBLISHING

Copyright © 2010 by Scott Kriner

ISBN 0-7414-6129-3

Printed in the United States of America

Published August 2010

INFINITY PUBLISHING
1094 New DeHaven Street, Suite 100
West Conshohocken, PA 19428-2713
Toll-free (877) BUY BOOK
Local Phone (610) 941-9999
Fax (610) 941-9959
Info@buybooksontheweb.com
www.buybooksontheweb.com

Dedication

This is dedicated to all of the people who were there for me when I needed them most during my medical ordeal.

To my wife who was my rock, providing unending optimism, love, care and support.

To my boys who unfortunately had to see me suffer through this, and for being understanding and caring while I struggled with the fact that I couldn't do things with them like I had done in the past.

To my parents and in-laws for their love, their help with the driving to and from doctors' offices, to the pharmacy, their phone calls, visits, baked goods and dinners during my recovery period.

To my Pastors and church family who prayed, called, visited, emailed, and sent cards wishing me well and praying for my healing and strengthening.

To my friends and business colleagues who really stepped up to support me, to encourage me, to check in with me, and to pick up the pieces while I was down for a while.

Contents

Prologue   1

Introduction   3

Foreword   8

Halloween   13

Floaters   16

Dr. Kraus   18

Follow Up   20

Telling Emily   23

The Retina   24

Operation Number One   26

Gift Basket   29

On My Knees   31

Oh the Pain, Oh the Agony   35

Quilts   37

The First Two Miracles   41

The Tears   45

The Angel   47

Operation Number Two   49

Second Opinion   51

Dr. Kim   53

Turning the Corner   56

Another Setback   61

Waiting   63

Operation Number Four   65

Pastors   68

The Breaking Point   70

Purpose in Life   72

Padre Pio   74

TITLE or TITTLE   76

Miracle Number Three   78

Shepherds in the Fields   81

Thin Spots   84

Operation Number Five   86

Another Tear   90

Operation Number Six   95

Cross Eye   97

What Was the Point?   100

How Much Longer?   103

Wait and See   106

Another Operation?   111

Prayers   113

Prologue

Life is a funny thing. Sometimes events are falling into place and everything seems perfect when suddenly a crisis of some sort occurs. We hear this from so many people, but many never think it could happen to us.

My life was like that. I had a great childhood. My sister and I were raised by parents in a small town in Pennsylvania. We attended church every Sunday, became part of the youth group, attended Sunday School, and went on to become active in our own ways within the church. Church life became just as important to our children as they grew up.

I am blessed to live and work near my parents and still attend my childhood church. My health had been good, and life was great. Then in October of 2008 a medical crisis changed my life forever. The events over the following years brought me closer than ever to God. The ordeal I went through was my cross to bear, and a real test of my faith. Thankfully, the support of family, friends, the church, and my wife changed my life forever.

One of the most important things that I learned was what it means to wait on the Lord. How we wait can be used as a positive step in a faith journey. As my Pastor told me, I had a choice as to how to handle my ordeal: Become bitter...or become better. I chose to become better.

Introduction

I do a lot of waiting – otherwise known as "traveling". I travel all over the country for my business. What I find most is that traveling is not simply getting from one location to another. It's more like waiting and waiting and finally moving from one point to another.

I wait in traffic heading to the airport parking lot. Then I wait for a shuttle bus to pick me up. Then I wait in line to check luggage. Then I wait in line for the security check point. Then I walk to the gate and wait for the boarding announcement. Then I board the plane and wait – sometimes for long periods of time- to take off. Then the plane finally takes off and I actually travel for a relatively short time. Once the plane arrives at our destination, I wait while the plane taxis to the gate. Then everyone jumps up at once and I wait to de-plane. Then I wait for the luggage to appear and once it does arrive I wait again to confirm my car rental reservation. Then I wait for the Rental Car shuttle to the lot. Finally, I then have the chance to actually travel a bit to the hotel, where I once again wait in line to check in. So I'm accustomed to waiting – not necessarily traveling.

As a child, my parents used a popular saying, "You wait and see" to establish their authority and knowledge on a subject. This was especially useful during the Christmas season as we all waited for Santa Claus on Christmas Eve. It was also a phrase used by parents to remind me that our parents had wisdom and experience in things that we did not have yet. So we needed to wait and see what happens on our own.

Children's faith and knowledge are not as fully developed as our parents. My sister and I never believed what they said would happen, but when they said, "you wait and see" it was like being told to humble ourselves, have faith, and we would see what we want.

Waiting has been part of our world's history. Scripture in the Bible talks about waiting on God in many situations. I started writing this story around the Christmas season when we all wait endlessly for the big day. By the time that Christmas Eve arrives, we look back on all of the shopping, decorating and partying and find it hard to believe that all the waiting is finally over. The Christmas shopping season seems to start earlier and earlier each year. As a result, we often forget the reason for the season – the birth of Jesus our Lord and Savior.

But think how hard it was to wait before Jesus even came into this world. For centuries prophets proclaimed that He was coming. The books of Genesis, Psalm, Micah, and Isaiah contain passages describing how and why to wait for God. The world prepared for a Messiah but kept on waiting. It was a test of faith and belief in the prophets. God sent the flood, but the people waited. The Jews suffered in Egypt where they waited to be set free. God's people were tried and tested over and over again but they still had faith while they waited.

Today we look back two thousand years ago and see that the waiting did actually pay off as Christ the Lord was born in Bethlehem. The world had to "wait and see" for this blessing to occur. Some say "good things happen to those who wait". For those early followers of Christ, they certainly saw and experienced good things as they waited and pondered this Messiah with such unorthodox teachings and simple lifestyle. But since his crucifixion and resurrection in that first century, the world has been waiting for his second coming again. This story helps us understand how to Wait on our God.

Our fast paced, horn-honking and instant messaging society is not comfortable waiting for anything. A two-minute breakfast in a microwave is often too long to wait for those hurrying to leave for work in the morning. We have express lines for those who can't wait to check out of a grocery store. We take our cars for express oil changes for those who can't wait at a full service garage. We use drive-through windows at fast-food restaurants when we can't wait to order food and consume it inside. We can even attend drive in church services on those Sunday's where we can't wait for a traditional service

This makes waiting difficult. We have no time…unless we learn to make our own time.

Our relationship with God is also too often in express mode. When times get tough we pray and we want instant results. We can't wait for His answer or action. We are disappointed when we ask God to help with a particular need yet the situation does not seem to improve as quickly as we'd like.

But God is a BIG God. He gives us strength to walk with him, as told in Isaiah – "My strength is shown in your weakness. My grace is sufficient for you." John Ortberg, the author of "If You Want to Walk on Water, You've Got to Get Out of the Boat," says that Christ gets "bigger" the more we trust him. If we really believe that God is always near and with us in the midst of our most difficult situations, it can change our lives. Sometimes, though, this means we have to wait on our God.

If we believe that God is with us always, then we know that we are safe in His hands. This makes Him a Big God to us. On the other hand, if we live our lives as if everything depends on us, worrying about everything, trying to fix everything by ourselves with no heavenly help, we are treating God as a Small God. We may know that He is a Big God, but the one thing that we don't know is the plan or the mission that God has for us. He, and only He, knows that plan and mission and He reveals it to us on his terms, and on his timeline – not ours. If we keep that centered in our thinking, then it becomes easier to wait on God for answers to our prayers.

As this manuscript is being finished for printing, my story continues. I now wait to find out if my medical procedures are nearing an end. How will this all end ? I guess I will have to "Wait and See".

Foreword

God provides us with countless opportunities to allow Him to touch our lives and change us. These opportunities may be there much of the time but we don't always recognize the events. Sometimes it takes a major calamity or life-altering event to change us forever by bringing us closer to God. He always answers our prayers.. we just have to remember that sometimes His answer is "NO". He has us right where he wants us, and he knows what we need and when we need it.

Our problem is that we often mix up what we want with what we really need. Often what we want would satisfy our physical well being, but it's what we need that strengthens our spiritual well being. What we want is nothing more than a wish. But God is not a Genie that automatically grants us our wishes when we make them. Instead He has a master plan for each of us, which will play out on his timetable – not ours. He will work within us to reveal his plan for us.

This story is about God's plan and mission for me being revealed through a medical crisis that started on October 12, 2008. Through the physical and emotional struggles and challenges, I was brought closer to God. As we get closer to God we learn to obey God and we find a deep love for God.

My purpose in writing this book was not to have readers take pity on me, but instead, to challenge you to Trust in the Lord, to seek God's presence everyday and to realize that we need to learn to wait on the Lord.

To those who wait and understand His grace, your life can be changed for the better forever.

"Faith is daring the soul to go
beyond what the eyes can see"

Halloween

Ever since our boys were in Middle School we celebrated Halloween by converting the lower level of our house into a Haunted House. Actually, we shared the haunted house with our next door neighbors. Guests would come in our front door and have their wits scared out of them before leaving out of our garage side door and then entering the neighbor's house. We even printed flyers that were delivered to all the neighbors in advance of the Haunted Houses on Maple Lane.

Once a theme for each year was selected, we came up with drawings of each room of the haunted house, and determined how many helpers would be needed. Our boys' supplied the manpower by asking their friends to help. The tradition got so popular over the years that friends were asking if they could help months before Halloween.

The helpers would arrive at 4:00 pm, and dress into their costumes, have makeup applied, and rehearse any last minute special effects. Then pizzas were delivered for our meal before Trick or Treat began and the Haunted House started at 6:00 pm.

Preparations had started for the 2008 Haunted House in August. This would be my younger son's last haunted house since he was starting college the following fall. Our older son was already in college, so this was to be our final hurrah. Without the help from their friends it was impossible to pull off the haunted house and live up to our reputation.

Our theme for 2008 was the Hospital of Horror. It was to have an operating room with a live patient screaming as the surgeon was sawing through his abdomen and his legs would jump and shiver. We had a maternity ward with deformed mutant babies, a psychiatric ward for the deranged, and a morgue where strange experiments were taking place. Special lighting, sound effects, fog machines, and choreographed speeches and screams were the final touches. How ironic this turned out to be – the theme for that year's Halloween was based on a hospital – a facility in which I'd be spending a lot of time over the next two years.

Two weeks before Halloween, it was time where last minute touches and props needed to be placed in the converted garage. The day started like every other mid October Sunday. After attending church and breakfast with my wife, we returned home and I changed into my work clothes. I pulled down the stairs into the attic above the garage and proceeded up into the attic to start bringing down the boxes of decorations and supplies. Flood lights, fog machines, special lights, rubber body parts, fake blood, rubber rats, masks, props etc. would be needed. Our attic had just about as many Halloween boxes and supplies as Christmas supplies!

After a few trips down the stairs with the boxes, I returned for what was to be one of the last boxes to bring down. That one was in a hard to reach area, and it took some crouching and straining to pull it out of its storage area. Once it was loose, I pulled it toward the stairwell. It wasn't a very heavy box, so I picked it up and proceeded down the stairs.

When I got to the bottom and put the box on the garage floor, I noticed something strange with my sight. I shook my head, thinking that some spider webs had been hanging on my face. That didn't help. Strange looking black stringy images were floating across my eye everywhere. Something was terribly wrong.

Floaters

I ran into the house and called for my wife Emily. She told me to put some drops in my eyes because maybe the dust in the attic had caused the problem. That didn't work. She then told me to sit and rest for a while and see if it cleared up. I tried that, but it got worse. Finally after 30 minutes of suggesting possible remedies, it became obvious that we needed to get to an emergency room as soon as possible.

Our initial thought was to go the local hospital emergency room. But I didn't like the idea of sitting for four hours before being seen by a doctor. Our next option was a smaller EmergiCenter facility that handles basic Emergency Room issues but without the hassle and crowds of a major hospital. On the way there Emily and I speculated that the EmergiCenter may not have the sophisticated or specialized equipment for eye examinations. So to play it safe, we decided instead to visit Westfield Hospital. We had never been there before but had heard from others that it was a more casual and friendly alternative to the larger hospitals in the area.

Being there on a Sunday limited us to one doctor working the Emergency Room. After some preliminary tests were conducted and my blood pressure was taken the doctor began his questioning and examination. His assessment was that there was a high likelihood of some retinal damage. He was not able to do anything further except to call my personal eye doctor to see if I could get an appointment the next day.

The next morning I called my eye doctor's office to confirm that their answering service had received the message from the Westfield Emergency Room doctor. I was able to get an emergency appointment with Dr. Kraus. Dr. Kraus was an MD and one of the retinal specialists in the practice. I later discovered that he was the surgeon for retina problems, hence his M.D. credentials.

Dr. Kraus

Dr. Kraus may be a skilled physician and surgeon but his bedside manner was quirky. He was not much for conversing, and had no noticeable sense of humor. But his examination was thorough and precise.

The diagnosis was that I had suffered a tear of the retina between the retina and the vitreous fluid of the right eye. He said that it could be repaired with a non invasive laser procedure. Of course I thought that had to be done in a sterile operating room. But no, Dr. Kraus immediately took me into a room at the doctor's offices and proceeded to bombard my right eye with rapid pulses of the brightest light I had ever seen in my life, at close range.

The laser was "welding" together the torn areas. But the result of the bright laser treatment was a temporary loss of vision in the eye. For about two hours I was blind in that eye. Once the vision started to come back, it felt like the eye was swollen shut – as if I had been punched in the eye.

This was scary for me. But I would eventually find out that this was the least scary of what I was about to experience over the next 16 months.

After a day or two, things began to improve. The sight came back. The haziness cleared up. The floaters slowly disappeared. I felt like I had been saved by Dr. Kraus and this ordeal was about to end. All I had to do now was come back to my doctor in two weeks for his examination. From all outward signs, I was on the mend.

Follow Up

I arrived at the doctor's office and waited for my name to be called. Then the drops were added to dilate my pupils and I waited for Dr. Kraus.

I greeted him kindly and looked forward to a reassurance that all was healing nicely. After all, the symptoms were all positive as far as I could tell.

But as Dr. Kraus peered into my eye under high magnification and bright light, he muttered medical terms to the nurse in the room who was making notes to my file. At this time my medical file was very thin. I would have never dreamed how thick my file would eventually become.

After a lengthy examination, much longer than I thought would be necessary to proclaim me as being healed, Dr. Kraus sat back and pushed away the device on which my chin rests.

"Well," said Dr. Kraus, "unfortunately, the tear is repaired, but there is detachment taking place." The blood in the eye had dissolved but he discovered a larger detachment of the retina in the lower portion of my eye. He said that because of the size and location of the attachment it was something that could not be repaired with a simple laser procedure. Instead he began to lay out options available to me for surgery. I was numb while listening to the options. It was difficult for me to make an educated decision on which option to choose. Based on his recommendation and description of the situation and the odds of success, I chose the option of a Scleral Buckle operation.

While I was in Dr. Kraus' office the buckle surgery was scheduled for the following week at the Westfield hospital. I met with a nurse and surgical coordinator in Dr. Kraus' office to make preparations. The first thing to do was have high magnification pictures taken of the inside of my eye. Then there were the forms to complete, the signatures, and the nurses providing explanations of what was to occur.

The Scleral Buckle procedure is actually considered a form of brain surgery. I was joking with the nurse when I asked what my options were. Without hesitating she said that I had the option of going blind if I did nothing, or the option of having the operation. I realized at that point how serious this situation was. The thought of losing my vision was sobering and frightening.

I was told that the recovery period would be one to two months, with some pain and migraine headaches but the vision would be restored within several weeks. It is an invasive operation involving the attachment of a wide rubber band to the outside of the eyeball which literally buckles or kinks the eyeball and moves the eye wall against the detached retina. Through this ordeal I learned a lot about the inner workings of the eye.

Telling Emily

Emily had asked for me to call her at work immediately after my appointment with Dr. Kraus. What was expected to be a 30 minute appointment turned into a 1 ½ hour visit with the doctor and nursing team preparing me for the operation.

I called Emily as soon as I returned home. I was composed at first while talking to her. She was shocked and surprised to hear about the diagnosis. When she innocently asked if I was "alright" with this, my emotions got the best of me and I broke down in tears as I muttered, "I'm terrified". Of course, Emily also then trembled as well. This was the first time I cried about this situation, but it was definitely not the last time.

In her characteristic nature, she composed herself and quickly told me that everything would be alright and we were going to get through this. I later learned that after we hung up on our conversation, she cried some more. Our fear was real.

The Retina

The eye is an amazing organ and the retina is one of the more complex components of the human eye. We take our eyesight for granted. But the processing of reflected light being converted into signals to the brain is nothing short of a miracle of God's creation. The retina is a layered tissue that lines the inner surface of the eye wall. If we were to think of the eye functioning as a camera, then the retina would be the film.

The lens and other optics of the eye create an image of the visual world we see onto the retina lining. As light strikes the retina a series of chemical and electrical events results in nerve impulses. Those impulses move to the brain through the fibers of the optic nerve. In fact the retina is considered to be part of the central nervous system.

The retina is comprised of several layers of neurons interconnected by synapses. The photoreceptor cells in rods and cones make up the neurons that are sensitive to light. Rods function mainly in dim light and allow us to see in black-

and-white vision. The cones support daytime vision and give us the perception of color.

The retina tissue contains about 7 million cones and between 75 and 150 million rods. The total layered retina lining is less than 0.5 mm in thickness.. Light is concentrated from the eye and passes across these layers to hit photoreceptors. This triggers a signal to other cells in the retina. That signal then moves to the amacrine and ganglion cells and then reaches the rods and cones. The neurons that are energized by the light create the signal from the eye to the brain which results in our perceived vision.

Between the front part of the eye and the eye wall is a sack of vitreous fluid. The sack is attached to the retina. Dr. Kraus told me that a small percentage of the male population in their late 40s or early 50s are susceptible to this type of retinal detachment. I quickly pointed out that I was not quite 50 years old, but he said my age was close enough!

Even more amazing to me than God's complicated creation of the human eye are the medical miracles performed on retinal disorders every day by skilled surgeons and nurses.

Operation Number One

My surgery was scheduled for November 3 at 6:00 am. The night before I laid awake trying to figure out how the procedure would be performed. How in the world would the surgeon get behind my eye to insert the band, move muscle, and kink the eye in a controlled way? After several hours of worry and lack of sleep, I came to realize that I didn't want to know how the operation would be done. I just knew that Dr. Kraus felt this was the best option to pursue. I had to put my trust in him and in the Lord to see me through this.

At 4:00 am on November 3, Emily and I drove to Westfield Hospital to check in. I had never had surgery, and had never been admitted to a hospital before.

The staff was very nice, friendly and methodical in their work of leading up to the operation. After all my vital signs were measured, and I put on the gown in a cold preparation room, I was moved to a strange recliner chair. That chair actually doubled as the gurney. When it was time for me to be taken away, the chair was reclined completely and I was covered with some blankets. The attendant hooked up the intravenous drip contraption and started to move me out of the prep room.

I will never forget that feeling of being rolled out of the room, getting a kiss from Emily and watching her disappear into the background as I moved closer to the elevator. Would I ever see her again? Would I ever be the same again? Would this be the final procedure and would I really heal back to normal?

Soon I arrived at the room outside of the Operating Room. There the nurses did more checks and measurements of my vital signs. I was asked repeatedly for my name, what was to happen, who my doctor was, and on which eye I was being operated. They marked the eye with a permanent marker, which made me happy. I was concerned after hearing stories of doctors performing surgery on the wrong arm or leg. So this way at least I felt reassured that Dr. Kraus would remember which eye to fix.

While waiting, Dr. Kraus entered the preparation room in his street clothes. He greeted me, and assured me that everything was in order and I'd be fine. He told me that the procedure would take about 1-2 hours. Then he said he'd see me again just before surgery.

Then it was time to be rolled into the Operating Room. I was reclined again and all I could see while moving was the ceiling, and door openings of several rooms. Then as I was rolled into the final room I saw the equipment, the bright lights overhead, the nurses scurrying to plug in sensors, monitors, and covering me with warm blankets. It was very cold in the Operating Room. I remember hoping that Dr. Kraus would be wide awake and well rested. It was very early to be doing such a delicate operation.

I was asked to count backward from 10, and I can remember thinking of the number 8. But then that was it. The next thing I can remember was slowly waking up several hours later from the general anesthesia. I heard voices of nurses trying to get me to eat crackers and to try to wake up. They gave me saltine crackers to eat and ice water to soothe my dry and parched throat. I was slow to come out from under the anesthesia.

I learned that Dr. Kraus had spoken to Emily after the operation and told her that the procedure went well. He was pleased with the way I responded to the surgery.

The next day I had my post-op visit to have the doctors examine me for infection or problems. From a medical point of view, everything looked fine. The doctors were happy. Another visit was then scheduled the next week to be sure the healing was progressing as scheduled.

Gift Basket

I try to stay in control of my life. My job requires me to often have the final say on so many things. To suddenly be told what to do by doctors, to lose control over my destiny, and to be on the receiving end of what would normally be an offering from me was a real shock to me.

The day that the first "Get Well" package for me arrived at the door was surprising. When I got to the door the UPS man was already getting back into his truck to leave. I brought the package into the kitchen table and opened it. I first thought it was a floral arrangement. But it turned out to be a snack basket from the board of directors of a trade association which was my largest client.

On the surface, this was a very kind gesture on their part. I was serving the trade association as their Technical Director. The gift really hit me hard. I broke down and cried like a baby while standing over the gift basket in the kitchen. This was unbelievable that I was actually receiving this. I would normally be part of the group being surveyed as to whether or not the board should send to others who were recovering from surgery or illness. Now I was on the receiving end.

The thought of these people thinking and caring so much about me during this time was just too much for me to absorb. My emotions got the best of me and I wept openly for many minutes.

Things improved later that afternoon as I composed myself. But when Emily returned home and saw the basket, I had to repeat the story again. And again, I wept openly. But this time, I had her arms around me with strong hugs to comfort me. She reminded me how nice it was for them to think of me, like I had thought of so many others in the past with similar tokens of support. It was my time to receive and to give others the chance to give back.

On My Knees

As recovery progressed I began to see images but they were fuzzy. I expected this would be the case. However several days later these images included a black veil near the top of my sight. I called the doctor's office to report this change and I was told to come in right away.

After Dr. Kraus completed his examination I was told that the surgery had been unsuccessful in re-attaching the retina. Other areas of the retina were now detaching. Dr. Kraus said that there was another option available to consider. It would require another operation, but it would not be as invasive. I was told that the operation would not require as long of a recovery period as the buckle procedure.

One of the first things I did after arriving home from the doctors' office was to do some serious soul searching. My emotions were running wild. Should I be angry that this was happening to me? Should I question God about this? Why me? Why now? What if things never improved? What if I couldn't work anymore? What if something bad happened to the other eye?

What should I pray for? Well, I decided to get down on my knees next to the bed and ask God neither to heal me, fix the eye, nor to patch things up quickly – but to use this experience to allow me to get my arms around Faith. I asked that my faith be strengthened and made real to me. To allow me to get my arms around this concept that had been mentioned for years while attending church.

Church had been an important part of my life. I was baptized, attended Sunday School and confirmed at the same church. It was a church where my family's previous generations had attended and served well. My grandfather had served on Consistory, taught Sunday School, filled in for the pastor on occasion, read liturgy, and sang on the choir. My grandmother was a fantastic cook and baker. She spent countless hours in the church kitchen helping to prepare dinners for fund raisers. She also sang on the choir and served in many capacities.

My mother was raised at the church and served as Assistant Organist since she was 17 years old. After marrying my father, they both became devoted church goers and got involved in many activities.

I had served 15 years on the church Consistory as deacon and elder and two terms as president. The second term I presided over a $1.8 million capital improvement project where we renovated and expanded the church building. I also served as chairman of the Festival committee for 20 years, was the master of ceremonies for the Consistory banquet for 20 years, and served on many committees, task groups, and small groups. So you get the picture – I was no stranger to my church and its teachings.

But something was still missing. I read the liturgy during worship services each week. I sang the bass line of the hymns as my father had taught me. I heard the pastor's prayers of the people, and learned much during the weekly sermons and preaching. But there was an emptiness that I couldn't explain.

I couldn't really describe what faith was or what it meant to me. How it could be shared with others. Was it just wishing or hoping for the best? Was it blindly believing in something despite having no proof? What was it ? I needed God to reveal to me what is Faith.

My daily prayers to God seemed so irrelevant in my mind. I stopped to consider that this same God who I was asking to help me had created the billions of stars, planets, and moons in the universe. He had created undiscovered matter in the cavernous space. He had shaped the majestic mountains on Earth, filled the enormous seas, created the forces at work to bring habitable climate for thousands of creatures – and created man itself in His own image. And here I was as a lonely insignificant soul totally irrelevant to the mighty God, the Everlasting Father and the Prince of Peace.

How could such a powerful and omnipotent God become personal and come this close to me? I had been taught that He had unending and unconditional love for every one of us regardless of our color, background or track record. But could this love and forgiveness be called into action for me? Could this same God that I had been worshipping, praying to, and singing about for almost 50 years be called into action to really help me? This would truly be a new journey in faith for me.

Oh the Pain, Oh the Agony

*"Wait for the Lord: be strong
and take heart and wait for the Lord."*
– Psalm 27:14

After the Scleral Buckle procedure, I suffered excruciating pain from migraine headaches which often lasted up to 30 hours straight. The stinging and sharp pains that were shooting through my head were debilitating. The doctor had prescribed Percocet as a pain killer and suggested Tylenol with codeine if needed. My mother-in-law even gave me some of her older Vicodin pills as well.

The drugs were no match for the migraines. A combination of Percocet and ice bags (actually bags of frozen peas or corn) were my last hope to deal with the pain. Many nights were sleepless as I sat in the recliner in a dark corner of the family room wondering how much longer the shooting pain would continue.

During these times you can imagine all of the emotions running through my mind. The physical pain. The fatigue. The urge to get up and move, walk or exercise. The prayers. The questions of why this happened to me. The wonder of when the pain would ever subside. Fear of what is going on inside of me. Anger that this even happened. Hope that things would eventually be fine.

For the first time in my life I could not explain what was happening and I could not rationalize this. So I had nothing to hang onto except faith in God and my trust in His will being done.

In one of Pastor Jones' home visits, he told me that there are several ways to deal with problems. One option is to become bitter. The other option is to use it to become better. It appeared that my upbringing and growing faith was enough for me to choose the latter and use this to better myself. Our Associate Pastor, Pastor Willy, also told me to stop rationalizing or trying to explain everything that was happening. Instead, he told me to Let it Go and allow my faith to bridge the chasm between explanations and the mystery.

Pastor Willy's visits and phone calls encouraged me to continue to trust in the Lord to take me down the right path. The plan was not mine. The mission was not developed by me. But He would use me and use this situation to shape me and make me better. God had me right where he wanted me. I needed to trust in the Lord that all would be good and to wait on Him.

Quilts

Many years earlier my church had started a Prayer Quilt ministry for members who were in need of prayers for recovering from surgery, or healing from medical conditions. The quilts were hand made by a group of women at the church, and displayed nicely over small quilt racks in the Narthex of the church sanctuary.

On any given Sunday, there could be one to three prayer quilts with the name of the person noted and for what to pray. Members were asked to stop at the quilts, tie a square not in the thread that extended from the intersection of each quilt square, and pray for that person.

Quite frankly, for years I had walked past any prayer quilt. The idea of tying a knot to help someone heal seemed hokey to me.

When I was suddenly home-bound and missing weeks of church services, my sister suggested to me that I should ask for a prayer quilt. Once again I shrugged this off thinking that I'd be back in church regularly within a few weeks and there would be no need for the quilt. But then more and more set-backs took place and my weeks away from church continued to mount. I did miss Sunday services. Sometimes I'd get a CD recording of the service that I missed. I cried heavily whenever listening to those CDs.

Again my sister strongly suggested that not only should I ask for a prayer quilt, but I should be added to the prayer chain. Prayer had never been a mainstay in my life. Yes, while the boys were younger, we always said a quick prayer just before eating dinner, but that was the extent of my daily conversation with God. Maybe this was an opportunity for me to renew my interest in prayer.

So reluctantly, I agreed with my sister and she added my name to the prayer chain at the church. Emily also had my name added to prayer chains of other friends, and my Christian business colleagues and friends said they'd add me to their prayer chains. Suddenly I was on prayer chains all across the country and even in foreign countries. It was truly a humbling experience.

My sister finally convinced me that I should get a prayer quilt. She spoke to the pastors and they arranged for one to be placed in the Narthex. After that service our Pastor asked if he could come over to present the quilt. I agreed, but didn't understand what the big deal was. In fact, I thought I could just ask my parents to bring the quilt to the house after they left church that Sunday.

Around noon, Pastor Jones arrived with the prayer quilt. He sat and talked with me about my progress and the prognosis. He helped to lift my spirits and preached a bit to me about keeping a healthy attitude toward God. He reminded me that during suffering we are drawn closer to God and further away from the secular world. Then he rose and asked Emily and I to stand with him as we held hands, with the prayer quilt draped over them, and prayed for healing and strength to be restored to me. I wept openly like a baby. It was a very touching moment.

I thanked Pastor Jones for his support and his ministry during this difficult time. I told him that I couldn't get through this without him. But he reassured me that I could indeed get through this on my own, but his role was to minister and offer words of enlightenment to help me.

Later that afternoon I crawled into my recliner and draped the quilt over my torso and legs. Within minutes I sensed a feeling of warmth over my entire body. It felt like a thick comforter and several blankets on me at the same time. Yet the prayer quilt was quite thin and did not look like it would be that comforting.

Day after day I'd sit and sleep with that prayer quilt on me. I'd look at all of the knots, run them through my fingers and dream of the person who had tied that knot and wondered what they actually prayed for. It was humbling to think of the number of knots and the fact that so many people had stopped even for a few seconds to pray and tie a knot. That love, support and prayer was the source of the warmth and comfort that I felt.

The First Two Miracles

"Be still and know that I am God."
– Psalm 46:10

One day, while suffering through more pain in my head something happened that I can only describe as a miracle.

I can remember sitting in the recliner without the prayer quilt for some time. The pain was getting worse, despite the Percocet pain pills and the ice packs. For some reason I did not have the quilt over me, but it was folded neatly next to the chair. I reached down and unfurled the quilt before pulling it over me from my feet up to my chest. And as I pulled the prayer quilt from the footrest to my chest, the pain melted away as the quilt moved. After it was pulled up to my chest, the pain had completely disappeared in that instant. The power of prayer, and the warmth represented by the hundreds of prayer knots from friends and anonymous members, had melted away the pain for that day.

That type of thing did not happen any other time, but this one time was a powerful reminder to me that God was in control. It was certainly His will being done for a reason.

The days and nights of suffering with the migraines were tough. Daytime was spent in the family room recliner and/or the sofa while listening to soothing music. It was the early stages of the Christmas season so our CD player was stacked with Amy Grant, Michael W. Smith and other Christian singer's albums. The music helped me get through the days, and allowed me to reflect on the season of Christ's birth and light unto the world.

Lights were irritating to me and somewhat painful on my eyes, so the lighting in the room was very subdued. When Emily returned home from work she'd try to get me out of the dark corner of the room. But the darkness was comforting on my eyes, even though it was a bit depressing.

For several weeks, I sat in the recliner during the day, and slept in it at night. Some nights I'd move from the recliner to the sofa and then back again, depending on how much pain I was in. There were nights where I spent hours just pacing across the family room with ice packs or frozen vegetable bags held against my head to deal with the pain of the migraines.

One night in early December I had yet another migraine attack going on 12 hours. Despite another operation, the side effects from the Scleral Buckle procedure were still affecting me with migraines. I had just taken my dose of Percocet pain killers, returned to the sofa and laid down with the prayer quilt pulled over me. I tried to get comfortable, and the quilt did a good job of keeping me warm. But while laying on my left side, the pain was incessant. After several minutes on the sofa I can remember offering another whisper prayer asking God to make the pain go away. I can vividly remember speaking to God in my short phrases and saying "Prayers and Perc...Prayers and Perc." Of course I was referring to the hundreds of prayers represented by the square knots that had been tied on the prayer quilt for healing and strength by church members. The "Perc" in the whisper prayer was referring to the Percocet pain killers.

I was hoping to God that between the prayers for healing and the medicine I had just taken, He would take away the pain. However, I was not prepared for what happened next.

After the third muttering of this corny phrase "Prayers and Perc," there was an unexplainable bright flash of light in front of my eyes, and instantaneously the migraine pain that I had experienced for weeks since the Scleral Buckle operation disappeared. "What was that?" I thought. "Was I dreaming?" Did a light bulb explode? "Hey, the pain is gone," I muttered. The prayer worked!!

I remember immediately sitting up, thinking that something had flashed in the room or that I was imagining this. But there was no confusion about the lack of pain. God had heard my whisper prayer and answered it with a miracle that night. The migraine pains never returned following the miracle that occurred that night.

This may strike you as something I fabricated or added to the story to give it extra impact, but what I described actually took place that night. I told Emily about it the next morning as she was getting ready to leave for work. She hugged me, cried with me, and praised God for finally relieving me of the pain.

The Tears

"I waited patiently for the Lord;
He turned to me and heard my cry."
– Psalm 40:1

During the next months, I experienced so many emotions every day that I didn't know how to handle them. I found myself crying every day, especially when listening to certain type of music, or singing in church, or hearing choir anthems. Every song had a deep emotional meaning to me, and I could not hold back the tears.

Pastor Willy told me that I should not be afraid to cry since that is when we are most vulnerable and when God can do his best work on us.

I learned to pray better and to appreciate music more. I found time for quiet meditation and to be patient. Waiting on the Lord took on special meaning. I had to wait on the Lord for his timetable of healing, set backs, and challenges. Everything that happened along the way was not according to my wishes or timetable. But each turn in the road was there for a reason. Something good came about it, and soon it was clear to me that trusting in the Lord meant that I had to work within His timetable – not mine.

Our bodies are nothing more than tents while on earth. These empty vessels wither and die no matter what we try to do to prevent it. But our souls are strengthened, nourished and prepared for that day when we will meet the Lord. Our "life" is not measured by the number of breaths we take, but by the number of moments that take our breath away". Why are we not looking for those opportunities for growth and spiritual strength? We all need more breathtaking moments.

The Angel

After missing so many weeks of church, Emily asked me if I wanted to go for a ride with her to church on a Saturday to pick up our Market Day order. The church used Market Day orders of food as a fund raiser. We had been introduced to Market Day food while our boys were in school. We loved the selection and quality of the food. The proceeds were certainly for good causes, and our freezer always seemed to have some Market Day boxes in them.

I agreed to go along with Emily just to get out of the house and get a change of scenery even if it was only for an hour.

We arrived at the social hall and I walked up the stairs to the Market Day area. My sight was not very good at this time. I can remember the hustle and bustle of the church workers carrying orders for people, and directing them to the location of their items. It was all a blur actually, and I don't recall clearly seeing any one person in particular.

I wasn't really in the mood to talk too much about my situation. I felt like a freak with so many people goggling over me when they saw me. But in a moment, one particular person, Carol Ann, walked up to me with the most beautiful and radiant smile on her face and simply said to me "How are you?". Carol Ann is a short person but packed with unending energy. She is the principle leader of our church Youth program and seems to be eternally young at heart herself. When I turned to see her, and experienced that ear to ear smile on her face, I literally felt like I was looking at an angel.

I hugged her and answered quickly that things were OK but I had a lot of work ahead of me. She didn't have to say much more. I will never forget that angelic look on her face – a genuine joy to see me. Hopefully I returned the favor and she felt the same joy from me in seeing her. For almost two months I had not been in church, and amidst the sea of so many workers in the social hall that day, God sent this angel to cross paths with me, and remind me again how He works.

Operation Number Two

The next operation took place on the Friday before Thanksgiving. Instead of trying to re-attach the retina from the outside inward, this operation would attempt to move the retina from the inside outward.

This time the surgery was to be done inside the eye using microsurgical techniques. According to Dr. Kraus the vitreous eye fluid would be removed from the eye and replaced with a silicone oil. Prior to that step the retina would be attached with a laser treatment to secure it before filling the eye sack with oil to hold the retina in place.

The procedure was done in about an hour. Dr. Kraus told Emily that the surgery had gone well and I had responded very nicely to the internal laser treatment.

The recovery this time was a bit different. Since the retina had been re-attached with stitches and lasers, I was told to sit face down at a table for the next eighteen straight hours. That evening I sat at the kitchen table with my forehead resting on a small pillow. My wife and son fought over who would stay with me that night by sleeping on the family room sofa. I didn't think I could fall asleep that way, but I did manage to take some naps and sip water over the eighteen hour period.

After the time was up, I sat up and felt stiffness across my shoulders and back. But the soreness quickly went away. The reason for having to stay in that position was to ensure that the oil in the eye remained in contact with the retina by keeping pressure downward inside the eye.

I was unsure what to expect this time around. Dr. Kraus had said that some patients regain their sight within a day of this procedure. Some can even read the entire eye chart, according to him. By now however I had come to realize that I am not the average patient. I felt more like the Born Loser. If the doctors would tell me that 1 in 10 patients suffer from a problem, I seemed to be that one person. If 10% of patients develop problems or have unusual symptoms- typically I was in that 10% group. Well, someone has to make up those statistics I guess - but why me?

Second Opinion

After a week from the last operation I still didn't see any change in my vision. In fact I saw things that didn't seem normal.

I called to make another appointment with Dr. Kraus. I had a bad feeling during that visit. Dr. Kraus spent a lot of time looking into the eye. He was telling the nurse to note many medical terms, but they didn't make sense to me. All I knew was that he didn't seem happy by what he was seeing.

Finally he blurted the words that I had dreaded and feared all along. He said that unfortunately the latest operation had failed to force the retina to stay in place and re-attach. He described scar tissue on the retina as being the likely problem. As he described it, scar tissue can form on the surface of the retina. It is very tenacious and constricts onto the surface of the retina, causing it to pull away from the eye wall. The retina in its current condition was not pliable enough to conform to the shape of my eye in the back with the scar tissue on it. He suggested some other procedures, but was basically out of ideas. He suggested that I seek a second opinion.

I was given two options for my next procedure: The Hershey Medical Center which was about 1 ½ hours away, or the Wills Eye Hospital in Philadelphia, which was about the same distance. I had heard about the Wills Eye Center as providing the best eye care in the northeast. So without hesitation Emily and I agreed to get a second opinion from a doctor there. Dr. Kraus then recommended a young doctor by the name of Dr. Kim. The nurse took care of making the appointment for us.

I was lucky to learn that my Lehigh Valley doctors were affiliated with other retina specialists. Our choice of a doctor associated with the Wills Eye Center seemed like the direction in which God was taking us.

Our appointment was made for Friday of that same week. I was glad that we could see him that quickly. I was fearful of delays with a detached retina. Dr. Kraus had mentioned earlier that once a retina detaches it can completely detach and vision can be lost within a week or so.

Dr. Kim

Doctor Kim's offices were in an area of north Philadelphia which was somewhat easy to get to. It was not in the center of town so we avoided major traffic hassles. Emily insisted on coming along on my visit to Dr. Kim. I could tell that she was now getting worried about how serious this could be. She didn't let on, and she appeared solid as a rock to reassure me that all would be well and everything happens for a reason. Deep inside, though, she was churning over this ordeal.

After the routine of drops, pressure checks, sight check, and dilation, I was called out of the waiting room into the examination room. The same chart that I had seen countless times in other offices was hanging on the wall. It showed the cross section of the eye and all of its internal components. I also saw the same type of chair, high magnification viewing machine, same head gear with high intensity light, and same eye chart in the room. This was becoming all too familiar to me.

After waiting about ten minutes, in walked a young oriental doctor with a big smile on his face.

He introduced himself as Dr. Kim. He was pleasant, engaging, and friendly. Emily and I immediately felt comfortable and assured with his demeanor and knowledge. We were impressed with his thorough examination and confidence.

He explained everything that he saw and suggested the likely cause. His first words were that Dr. Kraus had done a very good job with the Scleral Buckle procedure and the second operation as well. Upon completing his thorough examination without hesitating he suggested a procedure that he can do that would be perhaps my last hope to restore sight in the eye.

He determined that scar tissue had been forming on my retina presumably from the number of tears and re-attachments that occurred up to that point in time. The scar tissue was preventing the retina from reattaching. The procedure he suggested would remove the existing scar tissue and attach the retina using stitches and laser "welding". He would also remove the fluid inside the eye and replace it with a silicone oil to create hydrostatic pressure acting to hold everything firmly intact.

During the examination Dr. Kim also noted that the lens in my other eye was cloudy and looked like it would eventually lead to a cataract. Great! Just what I wanted to hear. If we ever get the bad eye fixed, I'll have to deal with the good eye in short order.

Then Dr. Kim made an interesting comment. Since my bad eye's lens was already cloudy, he suggested that he would remove the lens in order to work on the retina better. He'd leave the lens out until further notice, but replace it with a temporary lens. Clearly his objective at this time was to get the retina permanently attached and then deal with regaining my eyesight months later. When I asked how soon we should do this procedure he replied that we should not wait. In fact, he said that he could schedule the operation within a few days.

So surgery was set up for a hospital within the Wills Eye Center in Philadelphia for the next Monday which was December 8.

Turning the Corner

The third operation took place at Thomas Jefferson Hospital of Neuroscience in Philadelphia, which is part of the Wills Eye Center. We were highly impressed with the facility and the staff. The equipment that I saw in the operating room, at least what I could see on the ceiling of the operating room while laying on my back, was impressive. I was used to the routine of all the preparation, tests, and questions. When I was rolled into the Operating Room I watched the ceiling panels and lights go by and watched the faces of so many assistants and anesthesiologists looking down at me.

What I didn't see but what I knew was also there was Jesus in his white robe and in all his glory walking alongside the gurney with his hand on mine. I could feel the presence after I whispered a short prayer asking him to be with me.

Following the operation, Dr. Kim told Emily that the operation had gone well. He had used the laser to etch away or scrape the scar tissue on the retina. He found more scar tissue than he had expected but it was all cleaned up from what he saw. He felt that I could have my post-op visit with Dr. Kraus in the Lehigh Valley for having the pressure checked and monitoring any signs of infection. After that we knew we'd be seeing more of Dr. Kim.

So the next day at 5:45 pm we visited the office of Dr. Kraus yet again. He was in his office where we had not heard many positive words of encouragement. Rather, our hopes had been dashed -failures had been noted and additional operations had been scheduled. We were not sure what to expect this time. I was scared to go into the office. Prior to this ordeal I had never thought twice about visiting the eye doctor for a check up. Now, I dreaded the visit to the eye doctor. What would he find that I didn't know about?

After the examination Dr. Kraus informed us that the pressure was good, the retina was attached, and the surgical procedure had been done well by Dr. Kim. He literally knocked on wood, crossed his fingers and toes to pray that there would be no further complications.

On the way home from Dr. Kraus' post-op visit on December 9 we passed a local church sign that said, "If God is your co-pilot switch seats". That church's sign always seemed to have a saying or quote that had meaning to me. This sign was to me more than a man-made sign. It was God's sign to remind me again to Let Go and Let God.

I had prayed to God to strengthen my faith and to make it mean more to me than just the words that I've read and sang over a lifetime in church. I didn't know what else to pray for. I didn't really know how to ask God to give me more faith or to know what that would feel like. This was far too big for me to carry alone.

Let's face it, even our currency reminds us that in God we Trust. Do we really? It's easier said than done.

I'm an engineer by education so I always like to know how something is made or constructed or how it works. It's for this reason alone that I cannot enjoy watching magic performed on stage. Without knowing how they do it, without rationalizing everything that's gone or understanding the tricks, it is just too frustrating to me and not enjoyable at all. In fact I actually enjoy watching the shows on television that reveal the secrets behind the popular magic tricks.

But here I was dealing with a potential life-altering situation and wondering how the magic tricks work. What could I do to prevent this from happening and getting worse? Then I would sit and think this is God's will. I have no idea why I need to know why. Maybe God has plans for me that differ from my plans which were to continue in the field of consulting in the construction industry and enjoying living in that area.

Maybe God wanted me to experience loss of sight in order to be a testimony and witness to the blind community. Maybe this was his way to lead me down that path so I could bring my story to others that are experiencing difficulty like this. Maybe God would restore my sight somewhat and allow me during this process to grow in my faith.

Certainly the outpouring of well wishes, gift baskets, cards, phone calls, visits, and e-mails from so many people even beyond this area of the country, was for a reason. One of my friends told me that I should not object or fret about all the outpouring from others. He said it is their chance to be my Christ – to serve me. It is their Christian duty and I should not block them from doing this. It gives them a good feeling to help others and pray for them. That friend, Bob, also described life through the example of sitting on the beach. He told me that most of the time the tide is going out, as you share and give to others. But sometimes the tide also comes in and the outpouring of others surrounds you.

This was evident in the number of prayer chains on which I was placed. From Minnesota to Dallas and from Boston to California, and from Georgia to Pennsylvania. Emily's secretary, formerly from Georgia, not only put me on her previous church's prayer chain, but also arranged for their coordinator to send me what they felt was the "perfect scripture that applied to my situation" which was a passage regarding Jesus.

For the next six days following the surgery, my vision was noticeably better than anytime following previous operations. I was encouraged by this. But then on day seven and eight, I started to notice flashers, flickers and strange twinkling. For anyone who has ever had eye problems, you know that these are bad signs.

I immediately called Dr. Kim's office to schedule an earlier post-op visit to find out what was going on.

Another Setback

"Be joyful in hope, patient in affliction,
faithful in prayer."
– Romans 12:12

Dr. Kim thoroughly examined my eye again and informed me that once again scar tissue had formed on the lower part of my retina. The good news was that the laser and stitching was working to keep the retina attached – at least for the time being. He felt that the flashing lights I was seeing were caused by the scar tissue contracting on the retina and affecting the light sensors in the retina.

But Dr. Kim was concerned about the amount of scar tissue that he saw so soon after the surgery, when compared to what was present at the time of the surgery. The plan had been to wait two to three months to allow the retina to be fully attached and healed before replacing the oil and lens. Now, we needed to closely monitor the formation of scar tissue in order to see if the timetable needed to be moved up.

More concerning was the fact that a detachment occurring within the first month would require yet another operation and set me back again.

My next scheduled visit with Dr. Kim was on December 23. After examining my eye as he normally did, Dr. Kim gave us the news that we had dreaded. Even though my vision was satisfactory and no dark lacey curtain had been seen there was another slight detachment noted on the retina in the lower part of my eye. This would require yet another operation to attach the retina once again. Dr. Kim remained optimistic that things would work out this time since there would be less cutting; meaning less scarring and bleeding. All of that would presumably result in less chance of scar tissue forming.

Waiting

"Yet the Lord longs to be gracious to you;
He rises to show you compassion. For the Lord is a
God of justice. Blessed are all who wait for him."
– Isaiah 30:18

Waiting on God does not mean we simply sit around sulking and complaining that our prayers are not answered. While we wait, God is at work, accomplishing something significant for us, but on His timeline not ours. During the wait, what we do, how we think, and how we feed our mind is very important. During the mornings, after-noons, and evenings of seemingly unanswered prayer, the Bible tells us that we need to keep the faith, have hope, remain joyous and trust in Him.

Do you not know? Have you not heard? The Lord is the everlasting God, the Creator of the ends of the earth. He will not grow tired or weary, and his understanding no one can fathom. He gives strength to the weary and increases the power of the weak. Even youths grow tired and weary, and young men stumble and fall; but those who hope in the Lord will renew their strength...

- Isaiah 40: 28-31

I thank my God every time I remember you. In all my prayers for all of you, I always pray with joy because of your partnership in the gospel from the first day until now, being confident of this, that he who began a good work in you will carry it on to completion until the day of Christ Jesus.

— Philippians 1: 3-6

You will keep in perfect peace him whose mind is steadfast, because he trusts in you.

— Isaiah 26:3

My God, my God, why have you forsaken me? Why are you so far from saving me, so far from the words of my groaning? O my god, I cry out by day, but you do not answer, by night, and am not silent. Yet you are enthroned as the Holy One: you are the praise of Israel. In you our fathers put their trust: they trusted and you delivered them. They cried to you and were saved; in you they trusted and were not disappointed.

— Psalm 22: 1-5

We need to feed our mind with these kinds of scripture passages and positive thoughts. This allows us to be "better" rather than bitter during trying times. Behavior like this while we wait can also draw us closer to the Lord.

Operation Number Four

The next surgery in my ordeal was scheduled for the day after Christmas December 26, 2008 at Jefferson Hospital for Neuroscience again. So we celebrated Christmas and the birth of our Lord with our families as was the custom. The Christmas Eve service took on a whole new meaning to me. The songs were more real, and they caused me to tear up with each verse. The message seemed to take on a different meaning to me. The joy and the true meaning of what we were celebrating was more real than ever before. And the time with family was cherished more than ever.

I had been through a lot already and I was no where near done with this. The uncertainty of what I was facing was haunting me. Would I ever survive a surgery without forming scar tissue and future detachments ? Would I ever regain sight in that eye? Would my other eye remain healthy and at least give me something to hang on to?

The words of the season, Hope, Joy and Love, meant so much more to me. I was trying so hard to hope for the best. The repeated setbacks made

Hope that much more difficult to realize. But I started to think about my choices – worry about it, or let go of it. This is where I started latching on to the short phrases and whisper prayers that got me through the next fifteen months of this ongoing saga.

The day after Christmas we left the house at 4:30 AM for our 1 ½ hour drive to Philadelphia. We saw Dr. Kim before the operation that morning and he was more confident than ever. We exchanged pleasant stories about celebrating Christmas, and then he prepared for surgery.

My ritual was repeated yet again. The preparation, the IV, the questions, the tests, and the greeting from the anesthesiologists all progressed as usual. Then it was time to be rolled into another preparation room and finally into the Operating Room. The same sights of ceiling panels, lights, faces of the medical team, and the presence of Jesus at my side were part of the all too familiar ritual.

Following the surgery, Dr. Kim talked with Emily and reassured her that he had removed close to 100% of the scar tissue with ease. He told her that with any other patient he'd tell her that he was 100% successful. But by now he knew that I was the Born Loser and 99% might be the best I could expect.

My recovery from that operation followed along same lines as the previous operation. My post op visit with Dr. Kraus in the Lehigh Valley revealed good eye pressure and confirmed that the retina was flat and attached. My next appointment with Dr. Kim was scheduled for Tuesday January 6 and until then I was worrying everyday about whether I'd see the dreaded flashers and flickers of light prior to that next examination. I was still weak and fearful.

Pastors

During this whole ordeal I had the pleasure of periodically having lunch with Pastor Willy, our Pastor of Discipleship. He invited me to lunch at the local diner. Pastor Willy always seemed to have the right words for me at the time I was looking for something to hang onto.

On one lunch date, he described a Zulu African tribe that was hunting monkeys. The way in which they caught the monkey was to use a dried out gourd and to place a shiny metallic object inside of it. When the object would catch the light of the sun it would flicker and attract a monkey to the gourd. When the monkey reached down the throat of the gourd to grab the object it was too big for him to pull his arm out of the gourd and he was trapped. The monkey is not intelligent enough to know if he let go of this object that was meaningless he could be free. Instead, by hanging on to the object he was trapped and could not be free.

The life lesson for me in this story was obvious. I needed to let go of things that are unimportant in the grand scheme of things. I must let go of materialistic things, petty things and things we might think are important but in reality are meaningless. The best way to describe this is with the catch phrase that became popular several years ago- Let go - Let God. I also reflected on the saying "the best things in life are not things".

So what was important to me? What do I need to let go of? Well, my concern over falling further behind in my work was growing. I couldn't read emails or read printed publications very easily. I was limited in the time I could spend reading anything before eye fatigue set in. I certainly didn't want to over do it. At times, Emily would actually read my emails to me and I'd dictate a reply for her to send, or ask her to delete or save the email. My boys did the same at times. And I began using voice recognition software that my parents had actually gotten for me as a Christmas present before my eye problems ever started.

So I could let go somewhat. Interestingly, without spending every minute of every day on emails, conference calls, phone calls and traveling, the world did not come to an end. I did not lose my job. I did not lose contact with the world. And I DID have a chance to find out what was most important to me – I was growing in my relationship with God.

The Breaking Point

Several days after the December 26 operation Emily seemed to reach her breaking point. Since the very beginning of my ordeal she had never outwardly shown her emotions and concern over my ordeal. I knew this ordeal had to be taking a toll on her too, but there was never a sign. Instead she was the eternal optimist. "All was good," she'd say. "All was happening for a reason. I'd be OK. Things will work out. Things could be worse. Look at what you do have." This was her personality in general. We balanced each other, since I am principally a pessimist living by Murphy's Law.

On that day between Christmas and New Years Day, she was sitting at her computer when I walked in to just say hello. As I stroked her hair and rubbed her shoulder I could sense that she was trembling. When I looked down I saw tears running down her cheeks and she pulled back from the computer. Now it was my turn to comfort and reassure her that everything was in fact going to be OK. "Yes, she said, but I just want you to be back to normal and for everything to be as it had been". With that we both broke down pretty hard and finally had our deep cry together.

Once the cry was over, we composed ourselves and resumed our roles as worrier and re-assurer. Through the tears of both of us we hugged and reminded each other that good will come out of whatever the outcome of this ordeal. To this day she reminds me and reassures me that this is all for a reason. I need to find the reason as God reveals it to me.

Purpose in Life

Our purpose in life was the subject of a small group program that our entire church had done the year before. It was based on Rick Warren's book titled "40 Days of Purpose". I learned a lot about others and myself through those small group sessions and Warren's book. I'm a bottom line type of person who looks for the summarizing catch phrase or take-away point of any complicated subject. In this case, I learned that our main purpose in life is simply to put a smile on God's face.

We all know how to do that. We know that sin is nothing that makes God smile. We know that helping others, serving others, praising God, worshipping him, and obeying him are all things that bring a smile to his face. Doing the right thing when faced with choices is pleasing to Him as well.

The next months of my recovery were devoted to bringing a smile to God while moving further along in my faith journey. Things were starting to come together. I was almost getting my arms around this faith thing.

By forcing me to slow down in my life, and to take stock in what was important was God's way of re-focusing my life. It struck me as being ironic that God chose to use a vision crisis to help me re-focus my life. Suddenly I wasn't sulking about what was not working for me, but instead I was praising God for what he had given me. I could still see. I could still walk, speak, write, run, enjoy life, enjoy my family and friends, and enjoy my church family. I could still make a difference for God.

Padre Pio

Among the dozens of cards, phone calls and well wishes that I received during his ordeal I received a card from a colleague of Emily describing the Padre Pio spirituality center in Bartow, Pennsylvania. Padre Pio lived in the 19th century and died in 1960. He was canonized by Pope John Paul in 2002. According to Emily's colleague, many miracles had been reported by families who had visited the center. I felt that this was something we should look into.

We traveled to the center in Bartow and were impressed by the facility. A sanctuary and Chapel had been built in honor of the Saint who had performed miracles in the village in Italy where he lived before becoming a monk. The center also had a museum depicting his life with real life replicas of his home farmhouse and favorite areas in the Italian village where he prayed for hours on end. In one of the rooms, I saw a life-size statue of the Padre. As I stared into the eyes of the Statue I remember the feeling of wondering if there was anything of a miracle that could happen on my eye as well.

During the two hours that we spent there we prayed privately and together for much of the time. Emily and I knelt before the altar in the sanctuary and remained silent. But tears streamed down both of our cheeks as we prayed together. Neither of us ever asked what happened that day. But we felt that it was necessary. That experience of praying together silently strengthened our love and relationship forever. There was no reason to speak about it afterward. We have not discussed what happened that day, but I know it made a difference in many ways.

I can say that I prayed that day for the saints and angels in heaven and on earth to somehow find a way to lead me through this ordeal with an outcome that would somehow be good. In another room in the museum, there was a quote on the wall that said "your mission in life is known by but one... you must seek it out".

TITLE or TITTLE

I began to trust God. Pastor Willy, in one of his prayers with me over lunch, emphasized how important it is to trust God, Follow Him and Serve Others. That just about sums it all up, doesn't it? Everything that is right for us to do and everything that brings a smile to God's face, can be based on trust and obedience.

Looking for a catchy phrase that is easy for me to remember, I sat one day in my recliner and thought of an acronym that I could use to keep this thought in my daily prayers. What I came up with was TITLE – Trust In The Lord Everyday. Wow – that worked ! All afternoon I reminded myself of that new acronym that could remind me of this principle.

Later that same afternoon, Emily returned from work and suggested that we go for a ride and walk around the Promenade mall. This was a lovely Lifestyle mall near our home, with outdoor sidewalks and fire pits in use during the winter months. It was a cold December night, but I agreed to go just to get out of the house.

While walking through the Promenade shops, we turned the corner at a fire pit and I looked up at the only store sign I had really read that night. It was a sign above a sporting goods store. The name on the sign was obscure and I had never heard of it before. The sign read, "Shenk and Tittle". Tittle - not TITLE - but close. My eyes teared up at the sight of a version of my acronym that I had just created that same afternoon. Well it was slightly different from what I had developed as a reminder, but nevertheless I took this as a sign from God that he was pleased with my catch phrase. I stared at the sporting goods store sign and wondered what it could mean.

When we got home that night it became clear to me that my acronym had simply been modified for me. Now my whisper prayer would reflect on TITTLE – "Trust In The True Lord Everyday. This reminded me to remain focused on the only Lord we really have and to avoid worshipping other types of Gods like money, jobs, or career aspirations. My mind had to stay centered on those things that money can't buy.

Miracle Number Three

"The Lord is not slow in keeping his promise, as some understand slowness. He is patient with you, not wanting any one to perish, but everyone to come to repentance."
- 2 Peter 3:9

Eventually, when the migraines finally stopped, about three months after the Scleral Buckle procedure, I began sleeping in my bed rather than on the recliner. I'd pray each night, and each morning, that my faith would be strengthened. I also prayed some of the things that Pastor Willy and Pastor Jones had mentioned to me. To trust in the true Lord - to follow Him and to Serve Others. I reminded myself that this was His Will and not mine - and that the plan and mission for me would be revealed to me by God each and every day.

I also prayed each day that His healing hand would be upon me as the master physician and healer. These prayers continue today, in the morning and at night. More is added now, such as seeing the presence of God every day. And praying for those people and families who need to feel the presence of God in their lives for physical or mental healing.

On January 2, 2009, after saying my evening prayers, and putting in my evening eye drops, I fell into a deep and undisturbed sleep. I can remember looking at the alarm clock at one point and seeing that it was 5:00 am. I had several hours before the alarm would go off, so I nuzzled into the sheets and blanket for a good secondary sleep. But within seconds of getting comfortable, miracle number three occurred. As plain as day, and what seemed to me as a shout, I heard the words "I will heal your eye". It was a deep male voice, and clear as a bell. At first I thought I was dreaming. But I had just been awake and hadn't yet fallen back into a deep sleep. I also thought that it may have been wishful thinking and I had actually muttered the words in my sleep. But I don't talk in my sleep – even if I had been asleep.

Later that morning when Emily was up and getting dressed for work, I asked her if she had heard anything over night. She didn't know what I was talking about and said that it was a typical quiet night in the house. For me it was anything but typical. God had spoken to me in his own way. Pastor Jones has been saying for years that God is still speaking. The notion that miracles and God speaking ended two thousand years ago is just not true.

My experiences are proof of that, and I suspect many who are reading this book can share similar experiences. God is still speaking, in many ways. Our prayers are always answered – but sometimes the answer is "No". God has other plans for us. To say that we have plans is comical. We may think we have plans, but God has his own plan in store for us.

Shepherds in the Fields

Days after each operation I would sit with my eyes closed and look for flashes of light or floaters. I had grown aware of these signs of problems with the retina. I feared that they would come back each time. Every little flicker of light that looked unusual depressed me. I can remember whispering to myself, "Please not again…Please make these go away… Please make that one an exception and not to come back again."

But then I remembered the words that Pastor Jones and Pastor Willy had mentioned in an Advent Sunday worship service sermon. The message on that Sunday was based on the shepherds watching over their flocks by night when suddenly the angels appeared to them and they were afraid. But the angels told them "fear not, for God works above". In moments like that I needed to stop being afraid and instead Letting Go to Let God by trusting in the Lord with no fear.

Despite my physical condition and the poor sight, I managed to continue working at my consulting job. In February I attended a trade show as an exhibitor on the floor. I was able to talk to many people who stopped at the booth. Often they would comment on my eye, since it was obvious to anyone looking at my face that something was wrong with the right eye.

Those innocent questions about "what happened to your eye" often turned into lengthy discussions that revealed that these people had even worse stories to share. Whether it was physical ailments, their own eye problems, or physiological issues they seemed to revel in the chance to have someone who could relate to them to talk to. I was serving a ministry for them by allowing us to share our faith journeys and learn from each other.

Some had similar experiences with me. Some became blind after suffering through a Scleral Buckle procedure. Some started on the road to operations for detached retinas but then gave up at young ages, only to become blind in one eye. I even spoke to someone who had a scratched cornea that occurred from a patch that was placed on the eye during foot surgery! I was humbled by these types of conversations. I had been feeling sorry for myself, and yet I discovered that so many others had it much worse than me.

What this revealed to me was how widely people of faith are working side by side with us and we often don't even know it. Our daily conversations rarely deviate from the business of the day, and the fire fighting on the job. Only when we move those discussions to areas of our faith and our beliefs do we suddenly realize that others are starving to share their stories and support each other.

These discussions at a simple trade show revealed to me that people that I knew and those that I met for the first time were now praying for me, sending me mass cards, calling me later, and sending emails asking about my progress. This all occurred because I shared my faith which started with the physical effects of my eye problem. Again, had my eye problems not occurred these types of conversations with others would never have happened. Was this part of His plan? Was this meant to serve as an excuse to share my faith stories with others and allow others to open up to me as well?

Thin Spots

My post op visits were now being scheduled with associates of Dr. Kim in his practice. Fortunately they had offices in Bethlehem which avoided a long drive to Philadelphia for these relatively short office visits.

My next one was with Dr. Stottler. On both Feb 11 and March 25 I was told that my right eye, the bad eye, was healing nicely. But Dr. Stottler noticed that there were some thin spots on the retina of the left eye, which was my good eye. He said that eventually these would need to be lasered to strengthen the area since the thin spots were potential sites of tears or worse yet – detachments.

Suddenly the fear of losing sight in what was up to now my "money" eye loomed. At the time of the diagnosis, Dr. Stottler agreed that we didn't have to deal with this right now, but he went on to say that we didn't want to wait too long. What did that mean? Obviously he was concerned enough that he didn't want to put this off until next year. But it was not serious or urgent enough that it needed immediate attention.

Dr. Stottler recommended that when the time is right, I should schedule that surgery with Dr. Kim.

During my April 2 visit with Dr. Kim he concurred that my bad eye looks very good. I mentioned the comment from Dr. Stottler about the thin spots on the good eye. After Dr. Kim examined that eye he agreed with Dr. Stottler's diagnosis. Dr. Kim suggested that the next operation be at Wills Eye Hospital on May11. That procedure would fix the bad eye AND perform a laser procedure on the good eye while on the table. I wasn't too keen on this announcement, but then again who was I to question Dr. Kim's judgment. He had been wonderful up to this point.

Operation Number Five

My fifth operation took place at Wills Eye Hospital. The original plan was to replace the silicone oil that had been in the eye sack since December with a different permanent fluid. At the same time a new lens was to be inserted into the eye. I had gone without a lens and sight in that eye for almost 5 months. And finally, Dr. Kim was going to laser some thin spots on the retina of the good eye.

But plans are made to be broken sometimes. While Dr. Kim visited me in the preparation area, he expressed some concern and discomfort with the measurements that had been taken on my eye curvature. The device that performs the measurements is based on sound waves reflecting off of the wall of the eye. The silicone oil in the eye at this time was a source of interference with the sound waves and could give a false reading. Another complication was the fact that I had Lasik surgery on both eyes five years earlier, and this had changed the curvature of the lens area. And finally, the fact that I had a Scleral Buckle procedure earlier had changed the curvature of my eye ball itself.

All of those complications were enough to make Dr. Kim decide that morning that the precision of the measurements taken on site were not good enough for him to select the proper replacement synthetic lens. He suggested instead that we defer the lens procedure until I had a chance to visit a lens specialist. Instead, Dr. Kim would replace the silicone oil and do the laser treatments on the thin spots of the left eye.

I was at first disappointed and depressed that this would not be the last operation – I'd have to have at least one more. But I quickly agreed with Emily that if Dr. Kim was uncomfortable with inserting a lens that day, it was for very good medical reasons and we should not question his judgment.

On May 12 I had my post op visit with Dr. Fletcher, an associate of Dr. Kim. He said that everything looked good. There was no infection and the retina was flat.

The next day or two I started to see what looked like small oil bubbles floating in front of me. On Friday, May 15, I called Dr. Kim about the bubbles and asked if I could fly since I had some business trips coming up. He was surprised that there were bubbles there and he thought they'd dissolve. He did not think this would prevent me from flying.

However, that same night while driving, the bubbles and other floaters in the eye were getting to me. My eye felt sore, and as a result I chose to cancel the trip and not fly.

In the middle of May I was noticing that the bubbles seemed to break up into tiny specks. My vision was becoming hazy. It appeared like a snow globe but instead of white specs of snow flakes I was seeing hundreds of tiny dark specs.

On Monday May 18 I was seeing small specs, stringers, haze, and blurred vision. I hadn't seen this before so out of panic I called for an appointment and the Bethlehem office got me in that same afternoon. I met with Dr. Ortega. He did not see the oil, but said any remaining oil could move out of his sight depending on whether I was sitting up or laying flat. The good news was that he did not see any detachment of the retina. But the bad news was that he thought he saw what he described as a retina pucker. He described it as a wrinkle that sometimes forms after having the silicone oil in the eye for such a long time. It was similar to "pruning" of your fingers after being in the water for long periods of time.

When Emily and I heard this, we both assumed that this meant there was a new detachment. But Dr. Ortega said that the retina was not detached. To confirm his diagnosis, Dr. Ortega had me go into a different room for a 3-D ultrasound scan of the eye. The scan did in fact reveal a pucker. Ortega told me that the location of the pucker would interfere with my vision permanently unless it was removed. He described the removal process as one that is similar to a laser peel to level the area. He suggested that I wait to put the lens implant in until the pucker is removed. He felt that it would be better to give the swelling on the retina time to diminish and settle down. He also said that it would be possible to do both procedures during the next surgery.

Dr. Ortega also said that the stringers, floaters and small specs in my good eye were not blood. But I had a bad feeling about them. In fact to this day, Emily and I believe that he missed something in his evaluation.

Another Tear

My scheduled appointment with Dr. Kim was on May 21. I was actually looking forward to that appointment, just so that Dr. Kim could either confirm or refute what Dr. Ortega had told me.

I had my mother and father drive me there. It's a one- hour drive and my concern was having to drive home with both eyes dilated. That is not easy. After meeting with Dr. Kim and describing the same symptoms that I had discussed with Dr. Ortega, Dr. Kim started his extensive evaluation. This one was a bit different from previous visits with him.. He was using a tool that was allowing him to peer into the extreme outer areas of my eyeball. He was definitely looking harder and deeper than ever before. I was convinced that he suspected something that was out of the ordinary and more difficult to discover.

After his exam, sure enough, Dr. Kim told me that he had found a tear of the retina on the good eye. The haze, spots and stringers were actually blood in the eye from the tear. Yet Dr. Ortega had not seen this. Dr. Kim pressed around the eye socket until he pinpointed the location of the tear.

He then took me across the hall to the laser room where he immediately lasered the tear with a "welding stick" and magnification eyepiece while I was looking down at my toes as far as possible.

On May 28 I visited the doctors' offices in Bethlehem to see another associate of Dr. Kim. Dr. Fieri was the 4th of 6 doctors at that office that I've seen. Dr. Fieri found that the bad eye continued to look good, and vision was slightly better. He also said that the good eye with the lasered tear looked good. There were no new tears, the existing repaired tear was good, and he was pleased.

The next day while driving, I heard a radio evangelist telling me that no matter what is going on in your life, God has you right where he wants you. I also heard that we should be praying to God to have his way with you. I think that prayer was being answered daily.

On June 4 I visited Dr. Kim in his Bala Cynwd office. Everything looked good to him. There were no new tears in the good eye, and his repaired tear was looking good. He pressed around the eye a lot looking for anything. He felt that the bad eye was healing nicely. He said that he was happy with everything he saw. I was relieved and felt great to hear my surgeon tell me that he was happy with everything.

He then suggested that I see him again in 4-6 weeks, and in meantime I should visit with Dr. Akers – an ophthalmologist, for making measurements for my new lens implant.

On June 9 I met with Dr. Akers for the first time. He was a young clean cut doctor with an impressive demeanor about him. He was sincerely interested in helping me and promised to do everything he could to get the lens measurements as close to perfect as he could. He was up front with me, though, to describe the complexities of the measurement because of my history with the eye.

The Scleral Buckle was a complication. The Lasik surgery that I had done on both eyes five years earlier was a complication. And the damage to the retina over the past eight months didn't help either. After examining both eyes he told me that everything looked good to him. He commented that Dr. Kim had done a great job of keeping the compartment intact for him to insert the lens implant.

He said that his part of the next operation would only take five minutes to insert the lens. While examining the good eye, he confirmed that a film had started to form, as a precursor to a slight cataract. This is what Dr. Kim had told me after his first examination many months earlier.

The next step was for his technician to take me to several rooms where equipment was located. They took measurements on different machines and reviewed the data from my Lasik surgeries from my Lehigh Valley doctors. After reviewing the initial measurements, Dr. Akers was puzzled by some of the results. He took me into a room where he personally checked me on the machine again. After these checks of the settings on one machine were done, he was satisfied that everything was done correctly.

He told me that he would now take the measurements from the equipment, and do hand calculations and computer modeling to come up with the proper dimensions of this new synthetic lens implant. He reassured me that he'd come as close as possible to finding the perfect lens, but he warned me that there were other variables that might prevent sight to return to normal. I was prepared for that possibility and told Dr. Akers that if I needed glasses after all of this, that would be a small price to pay compared to what I had been through already.

Dr. Akers assured me that there was nothing that he could not address. In fact, if corrective eyeglasses were required, there was a chance that they might refer me to a pediatric optometrist where special lenses with prisms can often correct widely affected vision.

Later that day, I called the surgical coordinator to start the process of finding a date that worked for Dr. Kim and Dr. Akers to perform the next surgical procedure on me. The plan was for Dr. Kim to repair the retina pucker and Dr. Akers would insert the lens implant.

Operation Number Six

On Aug 20 I had my next operation performed at Main Line Surgery Center in Bala Cynwyd, PA. Dr. Kim and Dr. Akers greeted me in the preparation area and wished me well. They were both very optimistic. Dr. Akers told me that he had personally spent over 1 ½ hours doing math calculations and computer simulations to get the dimensions of the lens firmed up.

I was rolled into the operating room with some anesthesia underway. This time the experience was slightly different than in the past. I was not completely knocked out during the operation. Instead I was drifting in and out of consciousness. I could hear the voices of the doctors and nurses, and I had the sensation that my eyes were closed. But of course they were not closed. It was a surreal experience. There was no pain at all.

The procedure was completed in less than an hour.

Earlier, while waiting to be prepared for the surgery, we met Rachel, the mother of Jamie – a 10 year old beautiful girl having her 3rd operation. It was not to be her last. She had a strange accident where a small piece of metal spring broke off of a hair clip and went into her eye, causing her to lose her sight. The damage actually caused a retina detachment. I felt so sorry for her but knew exactly what she was experiencing with the full range of emotions.

We spoke to her mother and aunt before the operations. There were connections between both of them and with Emily and the people they knew from our area. Following the surgery, as I walked out of the waiting area, Rachel hugged both Emily and me and wished us well. Since then we have remained in touch with them via email. Unfortunately, Jamie's surgery that day was unsuccessful in re-attaching the retina. I pray for her everyday to keep the faith that things will work out for the better, thanks to God.

Cross Eye

I woke up the day after the operation, removed the plastic guard that I was to wear to bed for two weeks, put my eye drops in and looked in the mirror. To my horror, my bad eye was turned in toward my nose. It was a partial cross eye look. There was actually an image that my bad eye was seeing. This was the first time I had seen any image other than a blur of light, since December. But the image was terribly distorted and offset from the image I was seeing in my good eye. I feared that the bad eye would remain crossed forever.

Fortunately, the next morning was better. The bad eye had started to return to the center. The vision seemed to be getting better. The image from the bad eye looked like I was seeing everything under water. Vertical surfaces were wavy on the sides. Nothing was crystal clear, but for the first time in 8 months I could see some details on the television screen. Prior to that the TV was simply a blue hazy blur of light with no definition whatsoever.

Since the August surgery the offset image in the bad eye seems to be moving closer to the left eye image – but the progress is very slow with almost unnoticeable changes each day. The wavy outlines of things seem to be getting straighter but I might be imagining or wishing this in reality.

As of day nine there were no flashers or dark curtain veil to suggest retina damage. I've noticed that the bad eye's lid begins to droop late in the day as the eye tires. A big milestone was when I actually drove the car to the Promenade mall on a Friday evening. Because of the double vision, I chose to use my glasses with the right lens covered. But I found those glasses to be more irritating than without them. The false image from the bad eye is like a shadow. Somehow the brain is able to decipher between the good image of the left eye and the false offset image from the bad right eye.

On Sep 16 I had my follow up appointment with Dr. Akers. He was fine with everything he saw. The lens and cornea were good. He removed some sutures from the lens while I was awake. There was no pain, but a sensation of tiny threads being pulled from the eye area. It was scary but amazing that I didn't feel more than what I did.

He told me that the double-vision is normal and could get worse as the vision in the right eye gets better. Next time I see him he'll do a test to determine the potential of how well I'll eventually see. My next appointment will be in about a month. He mentioned that he saw scar tissue in the right eye, but the retina was flat. He admitted that he's not a retina specialist. This concerned me.

Based on Dr. Akers' comment on the scar tissue, I panicked and called to see Dr. Kim as soon as possible. My track record with the presence of scar tissue was not good and I needed Dr. Kim to confirm whether I was actually forming scar tissue. He had not seen me since the Aug 20 surgery so I needed the reassurance after his examination.

I made an emergency appointment to see Dr. Kim so that he could examine for scar tissue. The only available appointment on short notice was at the office in Tamaqua on Sep 18. Dr. Kim thoroughly examined me. Thankfully he found no new scar tissue. He felt that what Dr. Akers saw was scarring from all of the previous surgeries. The eye is beat up and shows scars. The left eye looked good as well.

Just to be sure, Dr. Kim scheduled another ultrasound 3-D cross sectional scan of the retina. The results from that scan showed that the pucker is gone, but there is still swelling. He prescribed a steroid drop and more Pred- Forte drops for the next month. He also suggested that when I see Dr. Fletcher again in October I should ask for another scan to compare to this one.

What Was the Point?

*"And we rejoice in the hope of the glory of God.
Not only so, but we also rejoice in our
sufferings because we know that suffering
produces perseverance; perseverance,
character; and character, hope."*
– Romans 5: 2-4

I often think about why this happened. What was the point? To change me? To give me a perspective that could help others? How can this help me to Make a Difference for God?

Sharing my story and attitude with others has resulted in others admiring my faith and resolve. Maybe this is part of the mission of the medical setback. Just when I start to feel sorry for myself and fret that the sight may never be the same as it once was, I am reminded of so many others who are worse off. Those who I pray for that they will feel the presence of the Lord during their ordeal which seems so much worse than mine.

I have a colleague who contacts me on a regular basis about my eyes. We share in our faith journeys and witnessing. I learned last year that he was diagnosed with a rare form of blood cancer. It was in the advanced stages which did not sound good. We've been in touch by email and seeing each other occasionally at trade shows. I later learned that his medication and other activities have helped with his prognosis. He is now feeling better, but still faces a bone marrow transplant, stem cell analysis, and massive doses of chemotherapy. And yet, in the midst of his anguish and fear, he finds time to ask how I am and to remind me that it is my attitude toward my eye saga that gives him encouragement and faith that he too will be able to retain a positive outlook. To allow him to choose to be "better" rather than "bitter". Maybe my attitude is rubbing off.

Others have commented that they admire my positive outlook on this. And yet I don't understand the dilemma. I don't have to struggle with it or fight every day to remain positive. My ceaseless prayer and conversation with God has made that attitude change possible. I have learned to Let Go and Let God which is another way of learning to Trust and Obey.

Jimmy Buffet sings a song about "Changes in Attitude and Changes in Latitude". Well, if we think about this, latitude is a way of measuring how high above the equator one is while on the planet on this world. The ultimate latitude is heaven, as high above the equator as we can get. Reaching to heaven will certainly change our attitude if we let it. The difference in this life-changing approach and the song, is that Jimmy Buffet is referring to a temporary vacation to a different latitude to change our attitudes. A heavenly change in latitude can permanently change our attitude toward others, toward God, and toward our purpose in life…to put a smile on God's face.

How Much Longer?

Another day and more drops for the eyes. Everyone is telling me that my eye looks so much better. The eyelid is raised and not droopy. The pupil is no longer dilated and appears to be center in the eye. This all sounds good, but my sight is not much better. Now almost 6 weeks after the August surgery and I still have double-vision with the right eye's image offset and angled from the left eye.

How much longer will it take to heal? I pray every day that God will lay his healing hand on my eye and repair everything. A friend has told me that he had double-vision as a result of a brain dysfunction. After several weeks of double-vision he awoke one day and it was gone. The brain had worked and worked to get the images of the two eyes to converge and it happened all at once. Would this be my experience?

The doctors continue to tell me that the healing of the lens and the reduction of the swelling of the retina will take months. How much longer will I have to endure this challenge to my sight? Will the sight ever come back to what it once was?

Will the retina swelling permanently affect the vision where the pucker once was? Will eye glasses ever be able to correct my vision and allow me to function like I once did?

But wait. Who am I to question this? We are told to wait on the Lord. All good things take time.. and we already know that the best things in life are not things. God works on his own time schedule based on what he knows is best for us.

Maybe if I was to wake up tomorrow all healed up, I would drift away from Him and feel like I don't need him anymore. Face it, when things are going great, we often feel like we don't need any help. It's when things get tough that we reach out for help from anyone. Maybe my growth in my faith is not mature enough yet to lift that need of mine to ceaselessly pray to him for his mercy and healing. Maybe my deficient sight is His way of constantly keeping me reminded of how frail the body is and how strong the spirit can be. Maybe the sight impairment will open doors for me and reveal another purpose or mission for me. Perhaps I am called to witness to those who have given up or who are tired of waiting for their prayers to be answered. Maybe this is a test of my will power to remain positive, faithful and filled with hope as an inspiration to others. If I can help just one person, I have made a difference for God. Is that my mission? Is that why I am being put through this physical challenge with no end in sight?

My next visit to Dr. Fletcher took place on October 27. The retina is still swollen which is interfering with my vision. Fletcher suggested that I continue using the steroid drops twice a day for at least another month. At that point, if swelling has not significantly dropped, a cortisone shot may be needed into the eye socket above the cheek bone. Until then, it's a waiting game.

I then visited Dr. Akers on October 28. My vision was no better than it was during the last visit. The swelling of the retina was masking the impact of the new lens. The lens looked fine. Dr. Akers' test for my potential restoration of vision showed a slight potential but it seemed unlikely that crystal clear vision will ever return to my eye. But until the retina swelling is removed, I would not have any reason to visit with Dr. Akers.

Wait and See

I met again with Dr. Fletcher on December 8. I had not seen any change in my vision – at least I thought I didn't. I expected to have another 3D scan of the retina showing little if any difference from the scan from the October 27 visit. The routine was the same. Check in, wait to be called for the vision test and drops for dilating. Nothing had changed, except my new cholesterol medication. But when the eye chart was illuminated and I was given the special mask over the eye, I could actually make out a blurred image of the letter E. And the next line had two letters that I came close in identifying, albeit blurred. I thought nothing of it, but I had forgotten that at the previous visit I could not even read the first line. I had been off the chart.

After waiting longer for Dr. Fletcher he came in and expressed some joy that there was slight improvement. No scan, I thought? How would he know that I'm making progress? It was the fact that I had read the first two lines of the chart. He did examine my eye and noted that the retina was flat, but the eye has been beaten up. I can only imagine what he is seeing inside a war-torn eye.

But the prognosis was good. He recommended that I continue to use the steroid drops, and increase the frequency to three times a day. He would see me again in six weeks.

My January 19 visit to Dr. Fletcher went like many of my previous visits. I had not seen any improvement in my sight since seeing him six weeks prior to then. I expected to hear him recommend staying with the Vigamox steroid drops for another six weeks and see what happens. During my eye test it seemed that there was no change from before. I could make out an image of one large number at the top. I guessed correctly that it was the number 8, but the two numbers below that line were too difficult to see clearly.

Sure enough, after the dilation and the pressure test of the eye, which I was accustomed to by now, I was called back to see Dr. Fletcher. His normal examination of my eye proceeded as he mentioned all of the "battle scars" he sees every time he looks into the eye. The good news was that the retina remains flat and adhered. The bad news is that the three months of steroid drops had done little if any good.

Another scan was suggested and I proceeded to the next room for the 3-D scan of the retina. After the image was printed out and Dr. Fletcher returned to review it with me, I quickly noticed that the bump seen in the image was an indication of swelling. Dr. Fletcher confirmed that as he described the printed image. When comparing that day's image to the two previously scanned images it was obvious that the swelling had not changed much at all.

So now we had new options to consider. Dr. Fletcher felt that the steroid drops could be discontinued since they had no effect on the swelling. The next most aggressive approach was to inject Cortisone below and behind the eye. A needle would be injected just below my eye in the eye socket above the cheek bone, and a small blob of Cortisone would be injected. The drug tracks along the surface of the eye and moves to the back of the eye where it slowly dissolves releasing the Cortisone into the back of the eye. This places the steroid closer to the site of the swelling and is intended to smooth out the wrinkled and swollen tissue. The risks were minimal, so I agreed.

The nurse took me to yet another room where she placed some numbing drops in the eye. After a few minutes Dr. Fletcher entered the room and dabbed some numbing agent on the spot where the needle would be injected. He told me that I wouldn't feel much pain and would not even see the needle being brought close to the eye. After I put my head back and was told to look to my left and upward, I felt the slight prick of the needle and within seconds the injected "cocktail" as Dr. Fletcher referred to it, was in its place and the needle was removed.

If this next step was to work, I would see results within the next four weeks. If I saw no improvement over that time, we would discuss other options according to Dr. Fletcher. Earlier he had mentioned that another option is surgery to repair the wrinkle on the retina that is stubbornly causing the swelling and the blur. After going so long without surgery I was suddenly contemplating what that would be like again.

But then, before I got myself too worked up again, I remembered who was in charge. I needed to Let Go and Let God take control. He would not be allowing the shot to take place unless it was for a reason. Dr. Fletcher was optimistic as he worked with me and mentioned that day that I was a young man and the "eye still had life in it". I was encouraged to hear him say that.

Another encouraging word from him was that during the mention of surgery he indicated that over the past year there had been some advances in retinal surgical procedures that improved the visual aspects of repairing wrinkles during operations. Dr. Kim had mentioned following the retinal pucker surgery that it was difficult to see whether the wrinkle had in fact been removed during the operation. From what Dr. Fletcher suggested, this uncertainty had since been improved on.

Of course the eye had life in it. The eye was the source of my renewed life in Christ. The whole saga starting in October 2008 had focused me on my prayer to strengthen my Faith. God was working through this ordeal using the eye, the setbacks, the victories, the pain, the tears, and yes the waiting. It was all part of His plan. There was much life in the eye.

The best news of the day was that my faith was kicking in and keeping me from fretting and worrying too much. Would things improve over the next four weeks? Would I have to prepare myself for another round of surgery? Would I ever see clearly out of the bad eye again?

I would have to wait and see.

Another Operation?

My scheduled visit to Dr. Fletcher took place on March 3. Very little improvement had taken place since my previous visit. Dr. Fletcher had another

3-D scan performed on me only to show a very slight change over the past five weeks.

We were running out of options. Dr. Fletcher felt that there was no reason to continue with the drops or Cortisone shot. The incremental improvement would not be enough to completely remove the swelling. Dr. Fletcher also stated that some of the reason for the blurred vision was some residual scarring and a wrinkle that remained in the retina.

Given the slow progress that I had seen, Dr. Fletcher mentioned that dreaded word again.. "surgery". A surgical procedure could be done to remove the wrinkle or scarring, and allow him to insert Cortisone crystals into the retina to directly reduce swelling and smooth over the tissue without scarring. I had never disagreed with my Wills Eye Hospital network doctors prior to this so why would I object to their suggestions now?

I agreed to the surgery with a sense of peace over me. I did not panic, or fret at the time. In fact, when the surgical scheduler and I compared our calendars, the first available date that worked for the surgery was actually April Fools Day. Would I worry about the surgery as we got closer to that date? Would this finally be the last operation that I had to endure? Would scarring continue to plague my recovery?

I have to wait and see...

Prayers

"The grace of God teaches us to say
'NO' to ungodliness and worldly passions,
and to live self-controlled, upright and godly lives
in this present age, while we wait for the
blessed hope - the glorious appearing of our
great God and Savior Jesus Christ."
– Titus 2:13

The ordeal has allowed me to grow in my faith. My prayer from November 2008 was answered. My family, friends, and Pastors had given me many nuggets of good information and biblical references to consider. These all shaped the prayer that I recite every day.

Dear God,

Allow me to please and praise you today

May your healing hand be upon my eyes this day.

Make me ever mindful to Trust In The True Lord Everyday, to follow you and serve others.

Help me to understand that it is Thy Will being done and not mine.

Have your way with me.

Reveal your plan and mission for me on your timeline.

And allow me to seek your presence each day.

Amen

Trusting and obeying our Lord are the keys to our faith. I don't know what the future has in store for me, and no one does. It has been two months since the April surgery and I still do not have clear vision. But no matter what shadows, fear or worry enters into my life, I know that I can trust in the Lord and obey His word. He tells us that He is always with us. So it's easy for us to reach out to him in those tough times.

He does answer our prayers for our own good. He works on a celestial timeline while we wait. But it is so important to behave properly while we wait. It's easy and human nature to become impatient, especially in our fast-paced society. But it is often the slow and quiet times when we feel God closer than ever to us. It is in those moments that we need to speak to Him, allow Him to speak to us, and grow closer in our relationship to Him.

As of the writing of this book my ordeal contin-ues. The swelling on the retina has not yet diminished. I have not visited with Dr. Akers yet to determine what if anything can be done with corrective eyewear to deal with my blurred double vision. However, my faith journey is based on my closeness to God and the impact that He has on my life.

And what is my reward for following Him and serving others?

Wait and See...